The Big Calls

Glyn Maxwell is a poet, playwright, librettist and teacher. His poetry books include *How The Hell Are You*, *Pluto*, *Hide Now*, and *The Breakage*, all of which were shortlisted for the Forward or T. S. Eliot Prizes, and *The Nerve*, which won the Geoffrey Faber Memorial Prize. His Selected Poems, *One Thousand Nights and Counting*, was published on both sides of the Atlantic in 2011, and his epic poem *Time's Fool* is in development as a feature-length film with Fox Searchlight.

On Poetry, a guidebook for the general reader, was published in 2012. *The Spectator* called it 'a modern classic' and *The Guardian's* Adam Newey described it as 'the best book about poetry I've ever read.' *Drinks With Dead Poets*, a fictional sequel, followed in 2016. Maxwell is working on a philosophical amplification of *On Poetry* titled *Silly Games To Save the World*.

His plays have been staged widely in the UK and the US. His opera libretti include *The Firework Maker's Daughter*, which was nominated for 'Best New Opera' at the Oliviers in 2014, and *Nothing* (also for composer David Bruce) which was nominated for the same prize in the Sky Arts Awards in 2017. He has also written libretti for Elena Langer and Luke Bedford, and for Mozart's *The Magic Flute*. His new version of Wagner's *The Flying Dutchman* premières in London in the summer of 2023 and will tour several port cities of the UK.

Maxwell has taught at the Universities of Warwick and Essex in the UK, at Columbia, Princeton, NYU, The New School and Amherst College in the USA, and now teaches on the Writing Poetry MA at The Poetry School.

First Published in 2023

by Live Canon Poetry Ltd
www.livecanon.co.uk

© Glyn Maxwell 2023

978-1-909703-41-4

A CIP catalogue record for this book is available from the British Library.

Contents

Acknowledgements

With thanks to Helen Eastman and everyone at Live Canon, to the T. S. Eliot Foundation for a stay in the Eliot House in Gloucester, MA, in June 2022, where much of the book was written; and to my past and present students at the Poetry School for their support; what I learn I learn by teaching.

I am particularly indebted to the following sources: *Sad Little Men: Private Schools and the Ruin Of England* by Richard Beard; *Breathtaking: Failures Of State: The Inside Story of Britain's Battle With Coronavirus* by Jonathan Calvert and George Arbuthnot; *Inside the NHS In a Time of Pandemic* by Rachel Clarke; the research of Hannah Al-Othman and David Collins of *The Sunday Times* into the death of Agnes Wanjiru; *Missing in action: UK leadership and the withdrawal from Afghanistan,* House of Commons Committee report; *Overview: The Police, Crime, Sentencing and Courts Act 2022,* the Network for Police Monitoring; *Grenfell: Value Engineering* and *Grenfell: System Failure*, by Richard Norton-Taylor, verbatim plays staged at Playground Theatre and the Tabernacle, and screened by Channel 4; reporting by the *Guardian,* the *Daily Mail,* the BBC, CBS and infomigrants.net on the Channel sinking of November 2021.

'Wreck' appeared in *The Times Literary Supplement* in December 2022.

*

Foreword

The idea behind writing poems that closely shadow famous work came to me as a visual image: the body of an innocent woman lying in water, otherwise known as Alfred Tennyson's Lady of Shalott. Once I had written 'Lady', the process evolved into a wider endeavour. The image that kept rising to mind was of weeds and flowers blooming from coffins, tombs or mausoleums, new life reaching out of structures built for the keeping of death.

I chose famous poems written at a time of England's greatest power and confidence in the world: the Empire years. And I mean England specifically, not Britain or Great Britain or the fabled, fracturing 'united kingdom' but *England,* and I mean specifically English *men*, who are the chief subject here, at least in the way their indifference, arrogance or violence has historically acted, and still acts, upon the world. I felt that by staying close to the rhymes or metres or simply the tones of these memorable works – some so familiar as to be almost inaudible – but playing new notes and chords upon them, I might grow or synthesize a voice which has its roots in victories, certainties, complacencies, but unfolds its new buds in the anxiety, corruption, division and darkness of England now. And I mean darkness, and I mean England now. There are many innocent deaths in these poems, and many English men. I'm one of them. The poems are written in a voice of English time at a time of English turmoil.

Yet whatever the poems say about England or men or time or myself, contained within the enterprise is a spirit of homage and honour to the original poets – Anna Laetitia Barbauld, Elizabeth Barrett Browning, Robert Browning, John Clare, Gerard Manley Hopkins, Rudyard Kipling, Christina Rossetti, Alfred Tennyson and Oscar Wilde – all of whom in their own ways sought the bright and largely abandoned grail of English verse: to write memorably, and by writing memorably to praise, to lament, to inform, to enchant, to attack, to remind, to warn.

'I met Murder on the way —
He had a mask like Castlereagh — '

Shelley, *The Masque of Anarchy*

Lady

After 'The Lady of Shalott' by Alfred Tennyson (written in 1832). The central events depicted in the poem occurred in 2012 in Nanyuki, Kenya. The facts are in the public domain and have been widely reported in the press.

The poem shadows the rhyme, metre and length of Tennyson's original.

Lady

On either side the river lie
long fields of barley and of rye
that clothe the wold and meet the sky.
Damn your thoughts and prayers say I.
       Meanwhile in Camelot:
the yellow-leavéd waterlily,
the green-sheathéd daffodilly,
shit grows exponentialily
       there. Forget-me-not

grows here with me. Those aren't the lines.
A soldier dozes, follows signs
around his school to where he finds
he must recite verse for his crimes
       then wakes and all's forgot.
Four grey walls, and four grey towers,
must have been asleep for hours,
shits and shaves, recites and showers,
       the Maiden of Shalott?

or something like, some Holy Grail
shenanigans, some foggy tale
of knightly passion, hill and dale,
one doomed and very very pale
       damsel in the plot.
He murmurs more: *in furrows airy*
'neath the moon, the reaper weary
something something, tis the fairy —
       Lady of Shalott!

Off the veldt a warm wind blows,
he can't think how the hell it goes,
failed it anyway Christ knows
a rose by any other rose
        out through the main gate. *What?*
he's shrugging to the guards behind
ne'er you mind, ne'er you mind,
none of your beeswax, think you'll find.
        Hey Y save us a slot.

     *

Not Y's real name. – Not far away
no time hath she to sport and play,
a curse is on her, if she stay
she's going to have to work today
        because it's all she's got.
She knows not what the curse may be.
This isn't even poetry
it's on your iPhone actually
        right-swipers of Shalott.

She lives with little joy down here
beside the water running near,
her baby's squawling in her ear,
she had better get her arse in gear.
        Stew circles in the pot.
The afternoon is thick and grey
her friend will come it's Saturday
when all the boys ride out to play
        from barbed-wire Camelot.

All the boys who'll never stop,
who take their orders from the top,
the land of bells and big it up,
ninety wars and one world cup
      O storied Camelot.
Sometimes through the mirror blue
the knights come riding two and two,
the lamps are on, the night is new,
      she's dabbing at a spot

for in her web she still delights
to weave the mirror's magic sights,
does Agnes, that's her name in lights
her real name, she pulls on tights
      and where's the friend she's got.
The time is past the time they said,
the lamps are on, the air grey-red,
I am half sick of shadows said
      the Lady of Shalott.

        *

To the appointed cheap hotel
our heroes stroll and where the hell
would you go? Soldier Y as well
and Soldiers Q and F and L
      and half of Camelot.
Sparkler vodka, Tusker beer,
the crowd is rowdy, night is here,
Soldier T will shed a tear
      and down a shot,

shudder then he'll take a bow.
We do know who, we don't know how,
some bloke's kicked off a major row
and Soldier X is ordering now,
              I call him Lancelot.
For one, he is a warrior bold,
two, his deeds have all been told,
three, this story's ages old,
              four, it's also not.

Five six seven eight and nine
o'clock O be my Valentine
boys of the Mersey Thames and Tyne
all lit by one green neon sign
              while women of Shalott
are driven up the empty lane,
the March wind blows across the plain,
ten twelve fourteen friends again
              dressed up in all they've got.

EQUATOR says the banging sign
they pass and pass a flask of wine
from south to north, they're there by nine
there there, there there, it's hammer time
              for knights of Camelot.
The air is smoke and yellow-grey
young ladies out on Saturday
so *too-rye too-rye fuckin A*
              carouses Lancelot.

              *

She left the web, she left the loom
she made three paces thro' the room
she saw the water-flower bloom,
she saw the helmet and the plume
            she look'd to Camelot...
sings Soldier Y and *what the fuck*
his neighbours spatter beer, *some book*
I did at school he goes and look
            he says, *look what the cat —*

or words to that effect. Just me,
some hundredth draft of history,
and not remotely poetry
but on your laptop actually,
            punters of Camelot.
Nanyuki, Kenya, so's you know,
the baby sleeps, the warm winds blow,
the baby wakes, ten years ago
            stew spoiling in the pot,

ten years ago the whole event,
X is living free in Kent
(not his real shire) the light is spent
and X is back from where he went
            and *what*, Y's shouting, *what?*
Help me, help me, X is crying
not shouting, crying as in crying,
gets his shit together sighing
            Killed her. That's what's what.

Lo and behold was Soldier Y's
response, who saw with several guys
behind the huts with their own eyes
a lidded septic tank where lies
       that lady of Shalott
for ten more weeks. King Arthur's knights
did tell King Arthur of these sights
but all were home within six nights
       in who knows, Aldershot.

      *

On either side the river lie
long fields of barley and of rye
that clothe the wold and meet the sky.
Damn your thoughts and prayers say I
       while Stacy stirs the pot.
Stacy's ten, her auntie Rose,
her real name, is hanging clothes
as off the veldt the warm wind blows.
       The mother who is not

lay there till June, a lad called John
smelt something in the morning sun.
Local inquest total? One.
Military enquiries? None.
       Knights of Camelot
interrogated? None. Inside
the Room D1 the night she died
one mirror, cracked from side to side,
       much blood. Forget me not,

I write and damn your thought and prayer,
the RMPs pound up the stair
arresting every soldier there
that night for what? for drinking there.
       Lawful Camelot,
they take their orders from the top,
the time goes by, the time of what,
two world wars and one world cup
       could pass in that sad spot

and nothing change. Diplomacy
makes nothing happen, just like me,
like thoughts and prayers and poetry
and anything we do for free
       in dwindling Camelot,
this infinitely shrinking isle
where you can zoom a google mile
to find the wines-and-spirits aisle
       where walks Sir Lancelot.

Last

After 'My Last Duchess' by Robert Browning (1842). The contemporary story is my invention. A 'murder wall' is the large poster that displays all the evidence in a homicide case, generally to be found in the field of entertainment.

The poem shadows the rhyme, metre and length of Browning's original.

Last

That's my last murder on the murder wall.
Not mine I stress, except in that it's all
mine, the case was mine, though I have since
moved on, it's my display, the sheets and pins,
the local cuttings, strings from clue to clue,
spaces on my wall for all these new
leads and hunches, for they come by night,
they do, I blink awake by the bedside light
then I battle to assemble that last dream…
Soon I'm smiling in the kettle-steam,
a wise connection made in the small hours.
No not the least decline in the old powers,
I'll assure my former colleagues, it's the case
we never should have closed. Her amber face
gleams in the dead centre of my wall,
attractive, at a do, so shy, quite tall,
holding a drink she hasn't touched yet, cheers,
I softly say and lift my mug, it's years
since all of this. Follow the dark-green twine
east of her picture to the railway line
where someone saw her walk, black marker pens
point to a capture from a dirty lens
down by the paper's edge: her friend, his dog.
Follow the red thread west to a house in fog.
Why did she go where she went, why did she do
the things she did? I know you, I know you,
I want to say but that way madness lies,
take it from me. I look in the bluebell eyes:
one day her prince will come. Does the station call?
Do they hell. Daresay their murder wall
lies flat in some wide oaken drawer these days,
I see it sliding out of view, her face
is pale, alarmed, *My case is closed? but why?*

You never solved it! Angel, so say I,
as I loop a silver string around a tack
and add a question mark, did she go back?
Don't go back, I whisper and my pen
rings a pencil sketch I made back then,
as best I could but not a pretty sight.
I stir my oatmeal as the early light
outlines the window. In one dream we meet.
I give her warnings then I walk the street
patrolling for the lady. In one dream
I'm leaping through the station to my team
to stop the drawer from sliding out of view
forever just in time! I tell them who,
and how and why and no one moves at all.
My lady rises from my murder wall
and then I wake. I didn't take this case.
Or any case, or worked in the police.
Or knew the lady or the pictures here.
Don't wish I'd done it let me make that clear!
But in some dreams I'm *known* of, have a name
that comes up in the briefings, in the frame,
person of interest sort of, and my files
lie underground on shelves that go for miles.

Journey

After 'Journey Out Of Essex' by John Clare (1841), a prose account of his escape from the asylum at High Beach, Essex, and his eighty-mile walk home, penniless and deluded, to Northamptonshire.

My story forms a companion-piece to 'Last', being the posthumous monologue of the victim in that poem. The diary shadows the voice of Clare's original.

Journey

<u>Journal Jul 18 — Friday</u>   I had come to an Inn and a place of
light I would say amber in colour   there one gave me a drink I did not
drink   for my freind got very sick from a drink given to her a week gone
by   but I did not want the man to be cross so I lifted the glass like
I would drink in time and I smild at him like I might be his freind in time
he said young lady   but there were no men there I would be a freind
of in any time I lifted my drink in any event

I remember how can I forget there was a young woman I would say with
an honest countenance rather handsome   I spoke to her and I
asked what party it was so she winkd at me and said it was a do and this
did make me smile so I tryed a joke with her and I said what do you at a
do and she went along with the joke and said no How do you do at a do
and soon we said in turn again and again How do you do How do you do
at a do   but this was before the man came who gave me a drink I did
not drink   for my freind got very sick from a drink given to her a week
gone by but I did not want the man to be cross so I lifted the glass like I
would drink in time

I remember in the door and out the window went a great green length of
cord that I could leave by and when I could not see the man who wanted
me to drink and when the handsome woman with her joke of How do
you do was gone I latchd on to the dark green hairs of the cord and began
to follow it away from the light of the Inn very carefull down the lane I
past the rough cord along out of my sore hands to guide my way as it
now began to grow dark apace the odd houses on the road   all were
lighted up I remember how can I forget

I remember going down a very dark road hung over with trees on both
sides very thick which seemd to extend a mile or two I did not know
where to go and all was dark in the way I was heading so dark I made
myself my company   and said How do you do and How
do you do like the young woman had said I said it first in my voice then a voice

like it was not mine but hers   so we could seem two souls together
when some time had past quite cheerfull I forgot the rough dark cord in
my hands and saw it was gone and could not see where it was falln all
being dark green and rough the same I remember I then forgot which was
North or South and though I narrowly examind both ways I could see no
house or tree or bush that I could reccolect I had past so I went on mile
after mile all most convincd I was going the same way I came   and
these thoughts were so strong upon me

I remember how can I forget I walkd down the lane gently when a man
came out with a light and eyed me narrowly I stopt to ask him if I was
going Northward and he said you have lost the cord and I said that was
true   he said that we all make mistakes and it is not your fault love
to be fair

when I said nothing back to him he said you are going Eastward to the old
rail way line he pointed me along the lane which looked cold and misty
now   he said it is very late for a girl like you   to be fair   you should go
back in to the Town or even stay a while here until you sort your self and
get your breath back

when I did not say any thing he said your eyes are like blue bells

I said they are not at all and he said oh yes they are and I said no for how
would I see any thing with flowers for eyes   and he laughd and I did
not and he said oh ho now we are getting somewhere   you
must stay and sort your self and get your breath back   I said no thank
you I am going Northward and I know my way from the old rail way line
he only pointed the way again and said no more   I remember
on the pale road were black shiney arrows I could see my way by and
they were leading me for want of any moon or stars or city light that
night how can I forget How do you do at a do I laughed with myself and
Much ado I cried and I wishd I could tell the woman when I see her again
in a corner Much ado at a do I would say   and as soon as ever I
thought of her I was in homes way

22

I remember how can I forget somewhere on the London side along by the
old rail way line the 'Plough' Public house all dark and misty now and
along the lane a man I know with his dog past me by   he askd me
was I lost and I did not want to say I was   I said no I am on my way
home   oh are you now he said which I remember how can I forget
oh are you now he said you can help me walk him and I will help you get
home   and as I stoopd and strokd the dogs fur I tryed to decide what
to do now as I knew I knew the man but not from where or when I knew
him no I said still stroking the dog and following its glosy fur along its
back no for I am on my way to my freinds and in my minds eyes the
handsome woman with the thing about Much ado   is waiting for me
there   she has put twin plates of bread and cheese and a glass of wine
out   oh really is that red or white he went

pardon I said   red or white he said   red I believe and he said I see
but you said you were on your way home didnt you at the end of the day
and I said my freinds home is my home we are One   and as soon as I said
that I felt myself in homes way and I stood up again   I remember
how can I forget he said Smile and I did not but it was too late to not and
there was a shutting sound like zip   he had took a picture of me
stroking his dog but I decided to pay no heed as may be he wanted truck
with me   so I said its a very nice dog I said I like its glosy brown
fur it has and he said where is your freinds house

I looked around I did not know where I was I said that odd house all
alone in the mist in the distance and he lookd and saw what I said was
there and there was a hap hazard trail of tiny red lantern lights going
down to it they were very pretty I was glad of them but he said thats
handy thats handy   why didnt you say you were only going there love

I said I couldnt see it at first in the mist but I can see it now my freind will be
waiting   with red red wine he said so very handy

23

and now I know she lives there dont I   then I was afraid for her and
about to say she doesnt know you she wont open the door   when I
rememberd in fact she doesnt live there at all and only in my minds eyes
so I made a cheerfull joke of him and said I dare say youll soon be best of
freinds and then

how many miles to babylon he said   as if I would be scaired and not
know the rime but I do know the rime I know very many rimes for my
long ocasional walks in the fields but I did not say the lines of the rime to
the man in stead I began my walk towards the house in the mist I wishd him
well although I did not look at him nor wish him specialy well

I sang to myself

"how many miles to Babylon
3 score miles and ten
can I get there by candle light
ay and back again"

and I remember how could I forget I did look back a ways to see if he was
seeing me still   and on the brow of the hill he was   and so was his
dog as if it missd me stroking it but at least the dog did not take a picture
I was joking to my girl freind in my mind as she is slicing the cheese by
candle light and saying why do you not pour the red wine   You   for
she calls me You which I love I must say

and I pretended that a light in the window of the house in the mist was
where she was waiting with the bread and cheese and wine   and I
pretended there even was a light in the window of the house in the mist

which there was not and to think she would be with me any where again
and call me You for the first time and last time call me You was also lets
pretend but I did so

I remember thinking how can I forget I pulld my self together thinking he
is still seeing me so I must pretend I would know the house of my girl
freind I walkd on with a purpose   I did hold my course and when I
got there to the dark porch with no light shining   I lookd back

he and his dog were gone I remember I then forgot which was North or
South and I did not know what to do except I sang some day my prince
will come   the song from the very old film

because I had been looking after little Jeany in the after noon for my
sister in the village to the North of the town and I saw that very old film
with her little one it goes

"some day my prince will come
some day we will meet again
and away to her castle we will go
to be happy forever I know"

it is His castle not Her castle in the film but I was thinking about my new
girl freind some freind You are I laughd being out when I need You and I
am hungry and tired   as I was walking away from her house she
did not live in I still smild at how mad it was to feel cross with her all that
wasting of food

I remember how can I forget the moon came out and it was sorry its too
late and I am lost the moon came out and made the narrow lane a silver
thread for me to follow

but to follow where for I forgot which was North or South and although I
narrowly examind both ways I could see no house or tree or bush that I
could reccolect I had past   so I went on mile after mile all most
convincd I was going the same way I came and these thoughts were so
strong upon me

I remember I kept asking myself the question should I go ahead or go
back it felt as if I had been asking that question for all of the time go
ahead or go back   go ahead or go back and along the road in the mist
I saw a tower I saw before I remember   how can I forget it is a
thin metal stalk of brass all the way to the top on high and the top is like a
hat but not a top hat a great wide circle flat hat oh but who ever can
climb up there for there is nothing to hold on to the cord goes
round and round and round it and goes away on its Journey

I got to there to the thin stalk I remember and waited there a time now
there was moon light and I could see my way I waited to decide should I
go ahead or go back and as I waited I sang some rimes I know   I sang
"How many miles to Babylon" and I sang "Some day my prince will
come"   and I sang a 3rd one a tune with no words

How can I forget far away there was a light through trees and I remember
I folowd the silver moon path to it and when I came through the trees
into the sight of it it was the car parking of an Inn and all the lights were
shining inside I would say amber in colour and at the door   how can I
forget there was a young woman there with an honest countenance
rather handsome I spoke to her and I askd what party it was so she winkd
at me and said it was a do and this did make me smile so I tryed a joke
with her and I said what do you at a do and she went along with the joke
and said no How do you do at a do and soon we said in turn again and
again How do you do How do you do at a do but this was before the man
came who gave me a drink I did not drink for my freind got very sick
from a drink given to her a week gone by

I remember in the door and out the window went a great green length of
cord that I could leave by and I latchd on to the dark green hairs of the
cord and began to follow it away from the light of the Inn very carefull
down the lane   I past the rough cord along out of my sore hands to
guide my way as it now began to grow dark apace and the odd houses on the
road   all lighted up and as soon as ever I saw them I thought I am in
homes way

Us

After 'Theocritus, A Villanelle' by Oscar Wilde (1881). This is one of many Victorian villanelles, but Wilde's is the particular inspiration because it calls upon Persephone, the maiden abducted to the Underworld by Hades. In Greek mythology she is the embodiment of spring.

My original title was 'News of the World', after the unlamented newspaper that was shut down in 2012 following the emergence of evidence that its journalists had hacked the cell-phone of a murdered child. The poem shadows the form of Wilde's original.

Us

In the dead air we wonder is she out there.
She should be here, she should have stayed on oùr side.
We listen to her gone and say let's go there?

We get there and get daffodils that grow there
growing there without her by the roadside.
In the dead air we wonder is she out there.

Her dog goes somewhere so we shout and shout there
we love that dog so much. He's still on our side.
We listen to her gone and say let's stay there

we need her so, there's nothing else to say there.
We sort the clippings till we find her good side.
In the dead air we wonder what she knew there.

We film the lilac ribbons in the dew there
and still she's twelve today. See it from our side.
We listen to her gone and have to be there

to the very end, set teddies by a tree there.
The mum, the empty bed, the tidy bedside.
In the dead air we wonder did she know there.
We listen to her gone, we do the show there.

If

After '*If* —' by Rudyard Kipling (1896). Kipling's poem was inspired by the life of the colonial administrator Leander Starr Jameson, perpetrator of the failed Jameson Raid (1895-6) in what was then known as the Transvaal (now part of South Africa) and his perceived maltreatment thereafter at the hands of the British establishment.

My poem is about the fire at Grenfell Tower in west London on the night of June 14th, 2017, in which 72 people perished, 85% of whom were from ethnic minority backgrounds, in the richest borough in the country. The poem shadows the rhyme, metre and length of Kipling's original.

If

If you would make an ugly thing look shiny,
        Or make an aged thing look good as new,
Or engineer a saving, though it's tiny,
        To suit the corporation hiring you;
If you would make it pretty from a distance
        Or come in under-budget by the date,
If you would hit your mark and meet resistance
        By never meeting it till it's too late;
Then you might turn your thoughts to aluminium,
        Or polyethylene, or PIR,
The cheaper stuff professional opinion
        Knows will burn like fuel but there you are;
And once it burns kill any who inhaled it,
        It being part-composed of cyanide
Or, if these compounds took a test and failed it,
        You might rename them slightly, let it slide;
Or, when the troublemakers make their trouble,
        Prolong the work or pine for luxuries
Like water-sprinklers, hallways clear of rubble,
        Lights that function, fripperies like these,
You'll hear them out but threaten legal action
        None can fight and if one night in bed
They all stay put because of an instruction
        Meant for buildings where a fire can't spread –
You're not alone, in fact you're one of many,
        Unnumbered are the ways to wink it through;
Some are convenience and most are money,
        Some what we did, most what we didn't do;
Ours is not the world and all that's in it,
        Ours is how we live and if we care,
Ours is everyone's last passing minute;
        Now you can't say you didn't meet them there.

Burden

After 'The White Man's Burden' by Rudyard Kipling (1897). Kipling's poem was originally written for Queen Victoria's Diamond Jubilee, revised as an exhortation to the United States government to colonize what was then known as the Philippine Islands, and sent in this form to Theodore Roosevelt.

My poem concerns the UK's disastrous flight from Kabul, Afghanistan in August 2021 in the wake of American forces. The poem shadows the rhyme, metre and length of Kipling's original.

Burden

And in a room there's this one
alone at work all day.
The embassy is roasting.
His endless emails say
help us sir, from judges,
translators, cleaning staff;
back home his mates in Hampshire
quote Kipling for a laugh.

Soon it's a room for these ones,
armed and in control,
the drawers all battered open
and any hopeful soul
who's penned an application
to work with the UK
should know it's being read now
and run the fuck away.

A dining room for these ones
in Somerset, in Crete,
in the Dordogne, it's August,
they're putting up their feet,
they're staying on staycation,
they're delegating calls
in sandals by the plunge-pool
as a whole country falls.

Will there be room for this one?
Time slows, a tiny child
is lifted over razor-wire
into the western world,
while far away on holiday
our leader leads the calls —
denied but well-attested —
to save some animals.

Will there be room for those ones?
an Airbus leaves the ground,
two hundred seats are empty,
guess what's London-bound.
By all ye cry and whisper,
By all ye leave and do,
The silent sullen peoples
Shall weigh your gods and you.

There was no room for this one,
no room on earth at all,
no room in heaven either,
time stops to watch him fall,
fall from help, from mercy,
a spot on a blue sky,
Pure is what his name meant.
Sod your prayers say I.

In a room forever these ones
with nowhere left to go
form half the population,
nothing you don't know.
Boys, you did your damnedest
the way you always do,
and it's almost always murder
and almost always you.

Mouse

After 'The Mouse's Petition' by Anna Laetitia Barbauld (1773). Her poem is likely to have been provoked by seeing laboratory experiments on mice conducted by her friend, the scientist Joseph Priestley, but Barbauld was a noted anti-slavery activist, so its scope is undoubtedly wider.

The Police, Crime, Sentencing and Courts Act passed into UK law on 28th April, 2022. It gives the Home Secretary the power to 'define any aspect' of the meaning of 'serious disruption'. The poem shadows the rhyme, metre and length of Barbauld's original.

Mouse

You caused him Serious Unease
        Discomfort and Distress
You caused Alarm or may have done
        Look at his Little Face

Your Demonstration did or may have
        Done that to this Mouse
It's up to me it's not a Matter
        For the House what house

Look at his Face you just Disrupted
        His Community
The Life of It you may have done
        Or did it's up to me

Or would you let me let Disorder
        Damage and Unease
Discomfort and Distress Etcetera
        Words resembling these

Govern here would you the Whole
        Community of Mice
Is weeping in my Mind's Eye make that
        All of Our Minds' Eyes

Or may have been to find they couldn't
        Have Mouse-cards today
When you all had or may have had
        Your terrifying say

Which may have caused him Serious
        Discomfort and Distress
He's gone without his Mouse-coins now
        Look at his Little Face

He went without his Mouse-rewards
        Or may have gone and why
Because you stood there Scaring him or
        Did in my Mind's Eye

You say you didn't Know you couldn't
        Do the Things you've done
You say you could've Yesterday well
        Crack on then crack on

You can't Today because you ought
        To Know or To Have Known
And you weren't able to Tomorrow
        Look at his Little Phone

With all your Faces in his Face
        This One like you is you
Or looks like you and if it is now
        What are we to do

To dry the Mouse's Tears the Mouse
        Is Weeping Join the Queue
God Save The Queen this Act signed April
        Twenty Twenty Two

Charge

After 'The Charge of the Light Brigade' by Alfred Tennyson (1854), which celebrated a calamitous attack made by British cavalry upon Russian artillery during the Crimean War.

My poem is a song of recent history, specifically the coronavirus pandemic as it impacted UK care homes in the spring of 2020. The poem shadows the rhyme, metre and length of Tennyson's original.

Charge

Home you go, home you go,
home where the home is,
take up your sheets and walk
grandma that's showbiz.
Plaudits the wipe parade,
clap for the chaps, he said,
suck up your sheets and walk
home where the home is.

Plaudits the wipe parade,
last night of Lucozade,
no one has plans for shit
no one can cope with.
These not emergencies,
these not the shade of these,
fly, pretties if you please,
cough up your sheets and walk
grandad that's showbiz.

Soap till what's left is right,
rinse till the day is night,
towel in the wilderness,
cope with and hope with.
Breathe like there's nothing else,
breathe till you rack yourself,
wheeze on your tod on earth,
mouth of a mouth of hell,
hole where the hole is.

Out on the garden there,
stranger to stand and stare,
mouth there to *there there*,
palm on the windowpane,
no going home with.
No going anywhere,
storm spreading round the chair,
screening of nothing,
forever and aftercare,
soap with and hope with,
home again home but home's
not where the home is.

Soap till what's left is right,
rinse till the day is night,
face at the window gone,
no going home with.
Breathe like there's nothing else,
breathe till you rack yourself,
wheeze on your tod on earth,
soon they're the shade of these,
soon only eyes are left
shocked through appliances,
nobody home with.

Why would you send them there.
What did you think was there.
Somebody's asking.
Asking for folks they know,
too late to tell them though.
Anyway. Asking

Memo

After 'In Memoriam, A.H.H.' by Alfred Tennyson (written between 1833 and 1850, to the memory of his friend Arthur Henry Hallam).

My poem charts the arrival of the coronavirus pandemic in the UK in the winter and spring of 2020, the government's response to it, and some reflections on the Prime Minister of the day. The poem shadows the rhyme and metre of Tennyson's original.

Memo

Mate, let's start with how this form
        was built for dwelling on the death
        of one beloved. One last breath,
one ended life, one life to mourn

*

unendingly. Let's start with why
        it's fit for that: a walking beat,
        iamb, *iamb*, alone on foot
and always soon the stop and sigh.

*

First lines so bright and clear they sing,
        a shift in thought and duck the rhyme
        we're free of fate! in double-time
we're here, not free of anything.

*

As I'm not free of you and you're
        not free of this. I call you *mate*,
        your name for me the only night
we met, I'm guessing '84

*

I might be wrong. The Balliol bar,
        you taking Classics with my friend
        I'd come to visit. In my mind
you're in black-tie, don't think you were,

*

then you're the mayor stuck on your wire
        with flags, then in a rumpled suit
        on Downing Street, you look like shit,
you're clapping – all I know for sure

*

is in the Balliol bogs the walls
        were inked with Latin banter. Whose
        or what I've no idea. Let's raise
the lid to little boys in halls.

*

But hey, world king, you didn't know
        your mate that night was one of you:
        world writer, call him, please – I knew
where I was bound and I still know

*

in spite of time and likelihood.
        Great Man Theory. How's that look
        these days, old lad? And how's your book
on Shakespeare? Anything you need

*

just ask me, I'm world writer... Mate,
        before I tell you how I think
        it's going, how it went, let's drink
to mutual greatness while we wait

*

for time to come, in our five-star
                abandoned overlook hotel
                where everything has gone so well
it's gone away. The land slopes far

*

below, we can't remember how
                we got here quite, we're only sure
                we booked ahead, we're catered for,
the afternoon was blazing, now

*

there's candles floating here and there
                somebody lit, the air is cool,
                we'll watch the sunset strand the hill
and wonder where on earth we are.

*

Mate, I do know where you were
                that Chinese New Year: Downing Street,
                poking lions to stimulate
a dance for all the cameras there

*

and where you weren't I also know,
                a Cobra meeting yards away
                on news from China. Good to see
that nation's in your thinking though

*

that January. One Dr Li
     with desperation in his eyes
     sends out a selfie, soon he dies,
and skiers are back from Lombardy

*

the worse for wear. The 31st
     you're booming to the Painted Hall
     you got it done, took back control,
four more Cobra meetings missed

*

and, mate, about the care homes: 'no
     transmission likely'? – February.
     You take a pregnant fiancée
on holiday, three weeks to go

1

till lockdown. As an expert says,
     we mustn't do things early. Mate,
     you're pumping hands and proud of it
in hospitals, your beaming face

3

should cheer them up, your Beano mop,
     you shake hands on a morning show,
     the only grin in sight. Swing low
to Twickenham, shake hands, play up,

7

and England win by three. Brave you,
 your rags declare. The evidence
 from Asia has no relevance
and these two experts think so too

12

or stand there while you say they do.
 The Races and the Anfield game,
 three thousand fans fly in from Spain
where everything has shut. Mind you

23

it's better to have caught the bug
 than never to be sick at all.
 Would seem to be the rationale.
Mourners never got that hug.

37

Blank days break. An eerie graph
 appears behind your tousled head,
 did you say what we think you said?
Squash the sombrero. Pause for laugh.

54

Pause to hold a baby shower
 at Chequers. Mate, I only ask —
 Operation, wait, *Last Gasp,*
you turn and smirk, cometh the hour,

cometh my mate. And now this flu's
      declassified by law, it seems,
      and not 'high-consequence', which means
less PPE's required. That's news

133

to nurses in their bin-bags. So:
      PROTECT THE NHS, SAVE LIVES,
      STAY AT HOME, three seers advise
from Friday next. Oh, Friday? no,

189

Monday, keep the FTSE safe,
      Monday March the 23rd.
      The army builds a mega-ward,
no units though or nursing staff.

303

Do wonder why so many went.
      We start to clap them anyhow
      and keep it up until somehow
it's time to stop. Just when I can't

592

abide your mug a moment more,
      mate, the virus tolls for you.
      I lie down, don't know what to do
with this, old boy. So pass a law,

1,153

do something. While you gasp for air —
   spoiler-alert you make it through —
   I sigh my sad heart out for you,
because I care, at least I care

2,720

for tragic cases. Which you are,
   mate. We know exactly who
   you thought you'd be one day, how you
kept up your crap impression, year

5,612

on soul-dejecting year. They all
   thought *him* a dick for ages, true,
   until his moment. Right on cue
your moment came, your hour, your call,

9,337

your Blitz, your Götterdämmerung
   came on a plane, came on a plate —
   your kind of wordplay, get well mate —
came with instructions. That's the thing:

13,593

points of light across the world
   had flashed their simple messages
   for months by now: *here's what it is*
and does, how it can be controlled:

16,551

here's what to do, what not to do.
          Data, numbers, black and white.
          Nurse Luis got his big call right.
Whether the same is said of you —

21,083

let's let your rags go toe-to-toe
          with truth until their race is run,
          let's see who wins that marathon
when all the loss is long ago.

24,852

Loss is never long ago.
          We've lost a lot since you showed up,
          mate, but that's just me, I'll stop,
take back control of what I know,

27,191

except I can't help wondering what
          you thought would turn out otherwise,
          would even microbes shield their eyes?
What country, friends, is this? — You're out,

32,992

you're clapping. Change of emphasis
          mid-May, not STAY AT HOME but STAY
          ALERT, and mate, there's one fine day
you're very much alert to this:

34,076

MEMO: sun is shining, team,
        how very hard we work, let's say
        we score some wine and cheese today,
BYOB, from 6pm!

37,723

This won't be known until the count
        is triple that, which won't be long,
        for in a few weeks everyone
is down the pub or eating out

40,597

to help out. Help out what? Somehow
        nobody gives the scientists
        you're following a hint of this.
More dead than in the Blitz by now

47,992

and two more lockdowns far-too-late
        to go. So went your chance to shine.
        Two years late they found a line
you crossed. Let's ditch the numbers, mate —

218,948

my bad. Let's ditch the numbers now
        and let it be. Pull up a chair,
        old lad, I never had to bear
the load you did. Didn't ask to though,

*

I might point out. You see that star?
        Our overlook hotel has five.
        Can't wait for waiters to arrive
but if they don't I'll find the bar

*

and help us both to drinks we like.
        It's lovely here, the valley falls
        away forever, distant hills
are green, are fawn, are gold, the light

*

is what I say. World writer, see.
        My memo's almost done, world king.
        Great on the vaccine, that's a thing,
a while at least. But PPE?

*

Enough. We all have mates. So cheers!
        Iechyd da and down the hatch.
        Anger hath a privilege,
a great man said, in fact Shakespeare,

*

so put that in your book on him,
        you've time to write it now, one hopes.
        We clink our glasses, watch the slopes
turn misty as the dusk rolls in

*

and still you're pumped and making plans.
       I guess I'll have to be afraid
       for both of us, world king old mate,
when down the darkened valley sounds

*

of loss and dread and doleful tongues
       are closing in the whole night long
       like Birnam Wood – then likewise strong
for both of us when no one comes.

From

After 'Sonnets From the Portuguese, 43' by Elizabeth Barrett Browning, popularly known as 'How do I love thee? Let me count the ways' (1850).

The words are taken either from that poem or from WhatsApp texts exchanged between serving Metropolitan Police officers, presented in evidence during their 2022 trial and conviction on charges of sending 'grossly offensive, indecent, obscene or menacing messages' under the Communications Act 2003. This group had included their colleague, a convicted murderer, though none of these words are his. The poem shadows the Petrarchan sonnet-form of Barrett Browning's original.

From

1

shithole. domestics back-to-back. can't wait
to get on guns. domestic violence victims
one thing in common women who don't listen
jon. I wanna test this theory mate.
hope to prove myself. to get a fight.
hope I get the only gay on section.
little fucker asked me for directions.
hounslow twinned with baghdad. that's alright
I've been an operator. lead me on
she'll get me locked up. dealt with one of those.
she'll use me sneaky bitch. domestics yeah
she's mental back-to-back. she'll use me jon
as an example. pretty good. there goes
pussy patrol mate. shithole. you'll know where.

2

pussy patrol mate. shithole. you'll know where.
the limit of my patch. end of the night
all shades of brown my life by candlelight.
god. old griefs my smiles and tears and yeah
I'm going to try and have a chat with her
the sneaky bitch she'll get me. put to use
I bet. ha love it. dealt with one of those
domestics back-to-back oh I went there
urgent assist those struggle snuggles jon
out of sight I pinned her to the floor
ah quality. a chat I'm going to try
and have a chat. can't wait to get on guns
and prove myself. get paired up yeah get more.
I'm just I'm feeling out of sight that's why

3

I'm just I'm feeling out of sight that's why.
level every day. my god I want
to taser cats and dogs to see which one's
the more pissed off I want to test this. my
mental ways jon. one was yellow asked me
directions he was lost. yep taser. same
with children yeah zap zap ya little. I'm
all my life I'm locked I would walk freely
by candlelight and sun I'm going to try
and have a chat. I'm lost. one thing in common
they just don't listen. women back-to-back
they don't. attention seeking jon that's why
and how do I. one thing in common women.
zap zap. my childhood mate. I bet the cat.

4

zap zap. my childhood mate. I bet the cat.
walking through it's like it's grace I lose.
end of the night shift. better talk to us
I want to listen try and have a chat
to my lost saints they love you. out of sight
they love you. shades of brown and one was lost
in hounslow. asked directions. you at least
jon your skill sets depth and breadth and height
I love you like zap zap. god love you better
mate I'm going mental. how do I
just get a fight to prove myself. can't wait
to prove I can. I've been an operator.
every day. our job. I'm going to try
jon mate don't listen try to strive for right

5

jon mate don't listen try to strive for right
it's getting near the end. I hope to prove
my faith all shades. I seem to lose my love
how do I every day. by candlelight
like going mental. I would have a chat.
walking with my lost saints ah my breath.
alright I love you. better after death.
jon you with your skill-sets back to back
use me love. that's that. my quiet need.
that's on the limit of my patch. if god
choose god choose the only gay on section.
count the ways god love you mate that's good.
that's good at least that still would be our job
yeah he was lost he asked me for directions

6

yeah he was lost he asked me for directions.
urgent assist. get me. those struggles. love you
mate all shades I'm never gonna ditch you.
no not ideal I love you with the passions
out of sight ah lock me up don't listen.
quiet need and getting near. zap zap
I can hear the call to love no lock me up
and lead me on. one thing in common. victims
you and I by sun by candlelight
purely victims. all my soul. I shall
prove myself and get paired up. I went there
the other week to hounslow it's alright
all shades when it's the end you hear the call
all out of sight you hear the call to prayer

7

all out of sight you hear the call to prayer
jon I love you mate like after death.
with my lost saints like love you with the faith
I seem to lose my breath and you'll know where
my smiles and tears. ah you know where they are
mate. I love you freely light and life
going mental to the floor with my old grief.
for love it's to the height and never more.
my cat and dog and girl and god and sun
and candlelight I call my soul. you hear
the call to prayer I do. it's every day's
childhood every day's direction jon
to praise to reach to strive love mate I'm there
I love you. how. let me like count the ways

Wreck

After 'The Wreck of the *Deutschland*' by Gerard Manley Hopkins (1876). The central events depicted in the poem happened in the English Channel on the night of the 23rd November, 2021. The narrative is based chiefly on accounts from the camp at Grande-Synthe near Dunkerque in northern France, and from the two survivors of the disaster. The 'dormitory' scenes are my invention.

The poem shadows the rhyme and length of Hopkins' original.

Wreck

Thou mastering me
who. I'm all alone.
There's no one there. For now I'll be
alone with Hopkins, one
alone with hope and dwelling on a wreck
along the coast of England. I've my own
and my own England too. I'll take
my form from his, the rest is English history.

First a sight
there'll never be, her gaze
enthralled by coloured changing light
in a familiar place,
my street in London late November, last
November, Christmas treat, a young girl's face,
a girl I know was never here, is lost
for good, I picture blissful by the fairy-lights

of Islington.
Her face shines pink then green
then yellow, soon it isn't there
and never was, and mine
is staring back. Or looking back, I know,
with this, or with this nothing-to-be-done
but this. I'm where she wished to go.
Least I can do is tell her where the place has gone.

Her name is Leaf.
It's not her real name.
It's what her real name means, I'll give
her family the same:
Pathright her mother, scolding her with cries
for dawdling by that window in a dream,
her brother Diamond rubs his eyes
and catches mine. His disbelief, my disbelief —

for no one's there
again, that's all I've got.
This Christmas crinkling in the air
is pretty much my lot
for wonder on the earth. But there they are,
Leaf and her mother, Diamond showing them what,
things on his phone, a tiny star
to light three beaming faces in a sea of trash somewhere.

Where. Dunkerque.
A camp out to the west
nobody wanted and it's cold and dark
save for the fires. The coast
nearby, the sea all afternoon's been calm,
the winter light is weakening. The least
thing I can do is picture them
and tell the picture who we are, who in the dark

at sea tonight
this very night will say
they're not our waters, just sit tight
and they'll send somebody.
Or words to that effect. That one effect.
Sixty years and I will have my say
on England, fond and fooled and wrecked
and sinking with three cheers in the dissolving light.

DUNKIRK. The kind
of thing you'd call a dorm
in the kind of school I have in mind:
TRAFALGAR, AGINCOURT,
DUNKIRK. The glory-in-excelsis, light-
in-darkness, heroes stumbling to the shore,
their England. Any year you like
the schoolboys in the kind of school I have in mind

dream of a world
long gone in the moonlit dorm.
I've known them young, I've known them old,
you know the voice. *KEEP CALM*...
They wait for the master's steps to clock and go
past twice more and be gone. They're a fourth form,
surnames start with M, N, O
why not, you know them old, you know them man and child,

you know the form.
A rich boy, Melivere,
will be the first to tell the dorm
to breathe, the coast is clear,
and he does and so they breathe, the master's gone,
then Melivere intones *There's no one here,*
now what the devil's to be done?
They mouth the words, they squeeze and wriggle to be warm.

Melivere
just sits and peers around
for shit to say and likes it here;
Maughm will get a pound
if anyone says one of seven things
forbidden on a whim today; Mills found
your diary he was hunting, sings
a song of *what I'm going to do with that, my dear.*

Myram shines
his torch below the sheets,
peeping at his homework lines,
shuts his eyes, repeats:
Kiss my hand to the dappled-with-damson west...
Kiss my hole, burps Noble as he greets
his cake that came today; still dressed
there's Nairn who talks in military call signs.

They're there because
they're there, to coin a phrase,
and England is as England was
those those-were-the-bloody days,
there there, nobody's there to say, and some
will sink and some will swim, nobody says,
or says the word, the word is *mum,*
the word wept under blankets in a world of loss.

No one speaks
to Opie in his bit,
his narrow bed that croaks and creaks,
all night he coils in it,
his breath in pieces; when a silence comes
they hold their own to hear him, breaking it
they piss themselves and wiggle thumbs
and shine a torch and mime the tears on cheeks.

I've known them
old, I've known them young.
The shittest stuff they do to him's
not far from what I've done.
From the dusty corner, from the empty bed
I try to meet his eye but we're long gone.
Lily and beast of the waste wood.
Banter, Opes, I wink in the darkness, only a game.

Dunkerque. *Again!*
Leaf pleads in the wilderness
to her brother Diamond on his phone,
he's trying to find her this
cool Christmas scene again with a shop display
and the coloured lights on a London street, it's bliss
to her, he says *we're on our way*
tonight, top secret, promise, they came back those men.

Diamond speaks
only what Leaf hopes
to hear, he's said the same for weeks,
he's said in their muddy steps
as they trudge back to the fires on their patch of trash
and munch their crisps between the rubbish-tips
and sagging tents. *Again? — No, hush*
he says. Leaf pouts or grins by how she rubs her cheeks.

Dunkerque. Twilight.
Soon, says Diamond, *soon.*
Darkness in the woods but light
across the sea. *Full moon!*
Leaf sings. *Not even close,* sniffs Diamond, *half,*
three-quarters — But you said this afternoon,
if it's calm tonight, it's a pond! cries Leaf,
an English pond... and she walks her fingers over it.

Sshh he does the same,
they play they're there, they meet
the Queen there (not her real name)
about where James Bond Street
meets Quality Street — *The lights again!* she cries
but he can't, *the battery sis,* she stamps her feet
to keep them warm and rubs her eyes
and whispers out to sea, he hears her — *like my dream.*

71

It isn't that,
Leaf, it's not the news
or is the news again but not
for you again, or yours,
Clandestine Channel Threat you were, they call
the new Commander that, they are fighting wars,
make mercy in us out of all
make mercy in us all or Christ I don't know what.

That Tuesday sailed
English-outward-bound
from Dunkerque: Leaf, Desire, Strong-willed,
Praiseworthy, Pathright, Flower-found,
Beloved, Helper, Rose-moon, Heaven-sent,
Fire-of-Honour, Mystery, Diamond, Friend
(not real names but what they meant)
and twenty more in a paddling pool that could hold —

couldn't hold. I,
Dweller-in-a-Glen,
am writing with my writing eye,
I didn't see it, one
Mohamed did (his real name to this day)
but I make a small voice cry — *the lights again?* —
as their plastic raft gets flopped away
onto the sea forever, out to the freezing sky

off Dunkerque.
The fourth form turn and sleep,
except for Myram's torchlit homework
squiggling in the deep:
where was a, where was a place, he's trying to learn
Hopkins for Double English, he's asleep,
the filament pink. Streetlights burn,
gaslights burn and candles burn in the age-old dark.

We're here because
we're here, to coin a phrase,
in England now and as it was,
these days, these boys' heydays.
Theirs never seem to end as heydays must,
but go on grinding history to haze
of Light and Right and Lord, the dust
I wipe and try to see my way through now, because

that winter's night
would find them all in post,
in power like Lord and Right and Light
blind-shining from one coast
to another. Out there somewhere the ship sails —
well Leaf calls it a ship, Diamond says *most
ships you call a She,* Leaf squeals
SHE sails! An uncle yells: *the cliffs are painted white!*

All turn to see,
Clandestine Channel Threat
they were, but the horizon's grey,
nothing to see there yet.
It's in his mind's eye like it's all in mine.
But someone saw it all and can't forget
so nor shall I. I mark the time,
my sixty years, my land, I'll have my fucking say.

Melivere. Hell,
if you know English sound,
you know the lounging fellow well,
he's played on his home ground
since he was born, and Maughm in the next bed
paid his dues to play there too, till he found
to his amusement what he said
went. Soon at the chime of the Division Bell

his was the call
that mattered. Mills shone too,
shone light where necessary, *all*
we do we do for you
was his nudge to readers every day for years
and Noble ate his cake as they egged him to,
got so fat his fat shed tears,
while Nairn stood sharp as always, stock-still by a wall.

There he is.
There they all are for good,
ruling the waves, the waves that rise
and plunge as the cries to God
go out again, a dot on an unwatched screen
their craft, while in the clear skies overhead
the wing-lights wink in red and green,
the dreamways of the deeply sleeping rest of us.

Diamond makes
a quarrel on the boat
sound fun to Leaf, his right arm aches
with clutching her, some vote
to turn around and some to hold their course
but the pilot says he's kidding there's no vote
and the uncle says he sees the shore
but he doesn't look to see this time and no one looks.

Rose-moon texts
her husband, Heaven-sent
his fiancée, the air-pump jerks
and rattles and is silent.
Praiseworthy (as his name means still) remembers
things like Fire-of-Honour (his name meant)
begging his neighbours *call the numbers*
(Praiseworthy trod the water, nine hours off Dunkerque)

now one hand bails
the sea and one hand holds
the hand beside, the engine fails,
the mother Pathright scolds
her Diamond always messing with his phone,
he's calling England's sailors — *Save Our Souls*
is what it stands for, little one,
the uncle teaches Leaf, *oh the big ship sails*

on the ally-ally-
O no one will hear
your song, I, Dweller-in-a-Valley,
promise you my dear,
where you are sailing to I have come from,
and I'm trying to understand — as a last prayer
howls from Pathright — where we've gone,
who you believed would help you. Down the gleaming alley

all green and red
Leaf runs to the magic window
in my mind's eye, our treat, our dead,
her cheeks go pink go yellow...
Thou mastering me, Myram, English don,
murmurs after class to his lawn-shadow
on the cricket field when day is done:
I feel thy finger and find thee, Lord... Praiseworthy said:

All night till dawn
they could take it. By the light
they let go one by one all gone
all went out in my sight
and english said french water there french said
english water no one came not right
not one more photograph please god
no this was the family oh, and there their little one.

Market

After 'Goblin Market' by Christina Rossetti (1859).

The story is my invention, but the poem shadows the setting, the rhyming patterns, syllabic structure and length of Rossetti's original.

Market

Morning and evening
always it's story time,
you or a man like you
come by, same time,
same cell, same story,
selling my wares I am.
Told you the best bit,
told you the rest of it,
look at your big book
bulging with clips of it,
thick with the gist of it,
fat with the most of it,
counting the cost of it,
reckon I missed a bit?
Dreamers together
in summer weather,
back to that day
we make our way
oh me, oh my,
the Fête... Everyone's there,
feast on summer Sunday air,
BEST KEPT OF VILLAGES
FIVE YEARS the streamer says,
some nights I dream of it,
last night, can't lie.
Still smell the smell of it,
heaven and hell of it,
why am I still here?
Why am I still here.
People do and people die,
you tell me why.

Morning to evening
the Fête was up and running,
also this long black marquee
folks had heard was coming,
strangers from the film world
stealing from their dreamworld
to cast us folks to be in their show
and all be famous! (I am, though.
Kind of, as you say.
Not for acting.) Anyway,
the black marquee was looming tall
and at the porch a bloke
calls *Come up when your name is called*
and all the village folk
come by, form a queue there
stretching down the dale.

All, I say, I mean the ladies,
they didn't need we gentlemen!
All the ladies in a line
stretching down along the dale
smaller till you can't make out
the faces at the utmost tail...
what. *Honey*. Who? *Ginger*.
What's the question? Them again.
Why do you ask that.
Both girls were there.
All in a summer light
to curl their sweet hair,
the ginger and the gold,
both born in this village,
aloof, the truth be told,
kept to their cottage.
Not on Sundays. Then they sold
their fads and foods and lotions,

their green and earthen potions,
they'd had that stall forever
and she there, the older one,
Heavenly Honey, her, whatever,
heavenly, people called her then.

What are you writing.
Not words of mine.
No Kemp's only quoting.
Cross out that last line.
Lose my composure friend and I don't want to,
not my intention, no. You say they warned you.
If they don't want to make Kemp mad
they shouldn't keep Kemp in here
night and day they should know that.
Actually we're done here.

                    *

Honey didn't want to queue,
Ginger pleaded, so they went.
I've agreed to talk to you.
We can put the past behind.
Kemp can if you can my friend.
Kemp's a reasonable man.

Honey didn't want to wait
hours and hours in blazing heat,
all the ladies helplessly
choose me, choose me!
Queue went winding on and on
all afternoon all sense had gone,
loads of them were drinking.
I've no time for drinking.
Loads of men were drinking,

signalling and winking.
Kemp has no time for that,
wished the girls well,
Kemp said give it all you got
they'll cast you all as like as not,
Kemp wasn't like the other lot,
Kemp had no wares to sell,
Kemp knew them girls from schooldays see.
You know I did, I know you do.
Honey had the eyes for me,
true and you can put that.
What's done is done, the angels say
and folks like you forget that.
The line snaked on,
they step up one by one,
the bruiser at the entrance beckons them in
and suddenly the meadows
are lonely with the litter and blue shadows
and all our girls are gone.

I *say* all, Jeeni's mates all day
were drinking by the brook,
she told them to stay put,
she didn't want them getting picked
in case she didn't, Jeeni.
She's like that. *Was* like that. Correct.
Was like that, was Jeeni.
One prowled in her bikini
made sport of Kemp which isn't fair,
no. Jeeni or no Jeeni.
Girls by now for a good while gone.
Our men fed up, all folded arms,
our boys alone with cups they won
that day and dogs were everywhere.
Ladies all showing off their charms

deep in the deep long black marquee.
Named it The Lot, we did that day.
I wonder when I'll catch the film.
You putting in a word for me?
You think they'd let me catch the film.
Why won't they let me catch the film.
I'm quite as famous as the film.
You fix that or we're finished here.
Since no one understands my pain
you understand. No one in here.
Because they're all insane.

                    *

All at once you hear this zip.
Afternoon turned evening.
Friends we're finished, step right up,
grinned the bruiser, bald and beaming,
all the b's, and like a flock
round the gap we swarmed, a pack.
We were lost without our beauties.
Through the flap and into dreamlight
ventured all the village through these
beaded curtains, mist and music,
twangling music,
you wouldn't even call it music.
Six threads of smoky limelight
each leading to a space
where darkly, face by face,
we recognized our girl-folk in that place
and all of them were there
I thought, with mirrors everywhere
like millions there.
We soon knew one was missing to be fair.

Let's leave it there.
I've said let's leave it there.

*

The Lot, we called them.
They weren't square shooters.
They said they wanted folks
but they didn't want folks.
No, taking us for jokes
they were, for losers.
They're not stuck here though.
There's only Kemp stuck here though.
Somebody call that fair?
They casted Honey.
It's Honey wasn't there.
One look at Honey
and bang. She's in the film.
I've never seen the film.
When will I see the film.
You'll ask them, will you, big of you.
They only wanted one of us,
one of us and she's the one they chose.
She wasn't there and all the ones who were
were asking is it her?
Who else was missing, who?

Amber ringlets, auburn hair,
knew that pair from days of school.
Honey was the quiet girl
and see what really isn't fair,
choked me up and always has,
chokes me up to tell you how —
Ginger was the girl for shows!
All she wanted in this world,

Plays! or films, she said in class,
Kemp can hear it plain as day,
Ginger in class in my mind's eye,
I'm there too, I see her now,
sat with me.
Ginger going *You'll hear of me.*
Ginger going *Don't laugh at me.*

*

Nothing's fair though is it.
You agree, that's why you visit,
find me kept in here forever,
days all chained together.
They were thanked for coming, though,
all the girls who'd had a go,
all the girls except the one,
Ginger asked them *where's she gone?* —
Photo-shoot, a man with sheets
patting Ginger as he passed.
She's the only one who's cast?
Ginger's murmured in a daze.
Help yourself to snacks and treats,
voice comes crackling from a place,
do help yourselves and see you at the film!
Kemp's not yet seen their film.

*

Soon everyone went home.
That Jeeni to her gang sat by the brook.
Kemp to a very cosy nook,
Kemp to his very home sweet home
they stole from him for what they say he did.
You don't believe it that's why you come by,

you're very quiet, I will spare your blushes.
Kemp knows the how and why.
Kemp knows they'll know the story by and by.
Kemp knows it's not goodbye.
Kemp'll have a street parade,
the girls will comb their tresses in the bushes
and all debts will be paid.

Poor Ginger packed their stall away,
they'd told her Honey had to stay,
obligations, costume fitting,
a star is born, they smiled.
Poor ginger child,
I'd have wrapped an arm around her,
that would have been my choice.
Soon the sun was setting.
Jeeni's screaming blue with her minions
Honey's famous, she'll make millions!
I can hear that voice.
Sat by a pylon, Jeeni's gang.
That sounds like thunder,
went Kemp the weatherman.

*

For days it rained as if The Lot
arranged it to, except that didn't stop
five hundred humble souls from showing up,
sat in the wet.
The days pass, the folks sit and stare,
you'd think someone would care
how Ginger was but Kemp alone was there
to do that duty.
I do call it a duty.
I was in fact a journalist.

I do in fact remain a journalist
however long I'm kept
in here to rot. You put that in your script.
I'm local Press.
And there was national Press
and international Press, the sun came out
one day and all the Press got summoned in,
the actual *Sun*,
the *Mail* and all to hear about
A Star is Born in England! *Times, Express*,
the *Mirror* and me too, *The-Dale-This-Morning*
that's me, I got my pass around my neck,
right here, they let me, look,
credentials, as they say –
yeah Kemp, he's in, they're nodding and turning
they wave me through *he's on the list today,*
that Kemp he's cool, he's Press.

      *

Lucky for them, lucky they did,
lucky they knew my name,
a local soul should always stake his claim,
he sees what others miss, he knows the score,
Kemp did, Kemp saw,
Kemp saw the beauty-queen brought in,
honey for hair and silk for skin,
they double-took, they did.
One look their minds were gone.
Not mine, I knew her, schooldays, do you see,
she had the eyes for me
ask anyone.

She sat up there, long table wedding-dressed
in bridal flowers, she said her shy helloes,
blushed to be there, sipped at a cup,
asked would she please speak up?
she did her best,
she said she did feel blessed
could she repeat that yes she did feel blessed
Honey are you an English Rose?
the fellow from the *Sun* wrote down, a bloke
was grinning *Don't suppose*
you're single? barely spoke
in answer. *Speak up please!* And them Fleet Street folk
they saw her shake her head,
man from the *Mirror* said
Hey Honey, how's it teaming up
with Maylo Brook? A smile
went everywhere, they waited quite a while,
she sipped her cup.

       *

Sorry, have to take these breaks.
It gets Kemp cross to tell it, makes
Kemp get the shakes.
I knew her, schooldays,
mixed emotions, me,
them teasing her like that,
Who's he? Who's he?
they'd say if Kemp raised up his hand
and had a question, *Who's our friend?*
they'd sneer. They would.
Third week or fourth I'd say.
That shut their holes, did they know who
the hell Kemp was? They would.

But suddenly it's half a dream
all eyes on me stood there.
The-Dale-This-Morning, Kemp's the name,
this lady fair
knows me of old,
if I may be so bold,
from schooldays, truth be told,
but I see no smile, her eyes stone dead cold
and that's their doing.
That's not the girl I know
from golden years ago.
Proud is the word.
She's said *Who's he?* and everybody's heard
her say it clear as day. She scarcely stirred
but no one said speak up that time,
I'm told they had their little laugh
and actually that is fine.

Can't laugh forever.
Messes with your breathing.
Messes with the weather.
Messes with the season.
Wait for it, Press-pack,
try and get your breath back,
Kemp is still breathing,
dreaming in flashback,
Kemp is dreaming always
coming down hallways
awaits at doorways,
miss me, you miss me?
it's not a dream it *is* me,
door can't help but open,
got your notepad ready?
how you gonna stop what happened,

gentlemen of Fleet Street?
Angels say it's done now.
Ask her your question
slick men beside her,
stole right inside her
mindset no question,
also Maylo Brook
famous young actor,
star of their dream,
leans to the lady,
elbow bare elbow,
look wins a look.
Folks are you dating?
Peeps you an item?
Kids get a room!
Kemp was drowned out,
drowned out by questions.
Switch it off. Get out.

*

Who's he? Not funny.
Who's Kemp? said Honey.
That's the selfsame Honey,
hard to believe now,
all for the money,
once had the eyes for me.
Head was all turned you see.
That night I'm walking
the dale and I hear talking,
calling me, greeting,
Funny us meeting...
Dale? – it's them Pressmen,
all my new friends,
national Pressmen,

Dale-This-Morning, right?
Watch the box tonight.
Played a blinder in there, mate,
Honey heart Kempo yes?
Something to share with us?
Cool, grab a beer with us!

Soft style, I told them, orangeade.
They make that for me here
but it's too weak and watery
so I told them I knew Honey
very soon there was too many
round the table, standing only,
they're leaning in to hear,
Mr Goldmine Dale! they cried.
I told them about Ginger
her poor forgotten sister,
all of them scribbling,
you Newshound Dale!
deep throat, deep cover!
poor ginga girl,
you done her ever?
School can we say?
they scribbled, poked at me
puffing their smoke at me
waved it away,
laughing, boasting, scribbling, toasting,
raise your glass to Dale-This-Morning!
Kemp's the name I said again.
Kemp's the name I've made it clear.
Day I'm out I'll say again.
I will be out. I can't be here.

     *

Nights her face shone everywhere.
Honey face and honey hair.
Honey's favourite this and that,
Honey tips and topics and fun,
tell-tale this and tittle-tat,
Kemp knows such is how it's done,
knows that now and knew that then,
Jeeni slouching in the sun
Honeygirls we are she goes
Honeytribe our time has come,
stepping out in Honey things,
smirking by their Honey-den,
swirl all night in underclothes,
Honey lace and Honey wings.

       *

One day nothing lasts forever.
Next day nothing lasts for long.
HONEY AND HER STAR ARE LOVERS
front page covers
WE'LL ALWAYS BE TOGETHER!
will you really? got that wrong,
got the paper,
bog-roll paper,
doesn't mean a shit to Kemp,
all them papers look the same
WHAT HAPPENED TO OUR GIRL NEXT DOOR?
SWEET INNOCENT SEDUCED BY FAME
and I was sad to read these words
some say there ought to be some law
but laws are only walls to Kemp.
Kemp never meant to hurt her
in word or deed or action,
she chose her path, she made her bed

them Pressmen started digging round
and things she's done or words she's said
like long ago somehow
who cares all sorts they found
each press reporter
and then it's all WHERE IS POOR GINGER NOW?
it's gone in that direction.

          *

Wasn't right what happened.
How'd you mean you know.
Go then, if you think you know,
be on your way, I'll bid *adew.*
You don't know what happened.
You think you know what happened.
Feel free if you do
to rot in here and I'll ride out,
I'm joking, friend,
let's swap our coats I'm joking friend
what friend I don't know you
I don't want to.
By now PROUD HONEY OR POOR GINGER?
all it was all about
by now, you had to pick your side
and sport your colours, sign in blood, decide.
That cunt or Ginger.

          *

I mean — *Honey* — beg your pardon.
Felt the moment.
Felt that moment.
Kemp loved both them sisters.
Knew them schooldays both them sisters,

shame on how the thing went down,
first the village then the town,
by and by whole country.
Whole thing makes Kemp angry.
Then one day and Kemp's not to blame
Proud Honey's passed and called for Kemp by name.

*

Night before the première,
pressmen there so you were there,
I was there
Mr Kemp I need a favour
Honey's told me in a whisper
Do this for me, for my sister
then you'll stay our friend forever
the way we were in old times
for we were close in old times
word for word, an urgent whisper
Please take this to our cottage,
she'll understand my message!
This, word for word
for Kemp can't tell a lie,
words barely heard
by that sly company
drawing her back behind the cord,
a small red velvet bag's been slipped to me.

*

Inside's an opal stone,
inside's a key, Kemp's on his way
off down the dale,
down to their cottage quick no soul can see
the path Kemp takes but he.

In old times we were close and those
are words she chose.
Kemp strides the dale alone,
down in the hollow there's their place
no light in any window. On the grass
outside six standing stones stir as I pass,
girls, six skinhead girls,
all changed, what have they done,
no Jeeni now but these are Jeeni's girls.

      *

Hair dyed red and then shaved, the sight they'd seen,
Ginger in that video shot
of dancing in some wasteland bar
they've seen, it's *Gingereens* they say they are
Are you a Gingereen
press scum or are you not?
Press scum! when my name is Kemp.
It's her sister's done her in.
They scrawled *GINGA* on my skin.
And I ask where's Jeeni gone
and they go *fuck knows who's she.*
Honeyscum.
Off they stumble in the gloom.
Door's wide open, Kemp can see
inside's all wrecked.
Light's not working, mirror's cracked.
Who would heal these wounds but Kemp?

      *

Who set to it.
That night all night and soon the dawn,
look at it all, the lounge all warm
white candles lit
for whomsoever comes. I made no choice
for what would be would be,
for I had sat until it seemed to me
I even said so, even heard my voice
advising me
go everywhere,
heal! I advise myself in my favoured chair,
am up the spiral stair
open to all that's lovely, to their rooms,
ever so softly to their rooms,
Ginger's so obviously hers,
Poor Ginger what a shrine was there
when Kemp was done, of dreams come true! of years
of fame of glorious years!
Kemp's pinned stuff everywhere.

      *

Days, weeks, months, years,
I don't know what you want from me.
I've not got any more.
You want to see Kemp cry some tears
for a mistake a travesty!
Nothing was in its rightful drawer
in Honey's room, things spread around,
the dress they say Kemp wore
was Honey's. Kemp was found.
Kemp meant to, we were close we two
she lied to you and men like you
and proud she was and for her pride
she stole poor Ginger's dream,

she took her dream and wolfed it down
and dwelt in far hotels with him
and woke together for weeks with him
she planned it, no one knew,
she planned it all apparently.
Plus what was done to Jeeni.
For in the dark Kemp couldn't know her,
Kemp must have thought it's Honey,
her scent and wig and dress the same,
what's done is done and who's to blame?
Poor broken angel Kemp bore down
the stairs so tenderly.

LIVE CANON